Original title:
The Living Room Chronicles

Copyright © 2025 Creative Arts Management OÜ
All rights reserved.

Author: Colin Harrington
ISBN HARDBACK: 978-1-80587-073-9
ISBN PAPERBACK: 978-1-80587-543-7

Comfort in Chaos

Cushions spill like popcorn, alive,
Remote's lost in a blanket dive.
A cat naps soundly, dreams of mice,
While socks argue, "We're not so nice!"

Coffee stains dance like little bugs,
And dust bunnies hold secret hugs.
The laugh track plays from yesterday's show,
As a pizza box steals the living room glow.

The Scent of Old Books

Pages crinkle like a lover's sigh,
Dust motes swirling, oh my, oh my!
Bookmarks lost in ancient tales,
As we sip tea from chipped porcelain pails.

A novel's spine creaks, like a joke,
Whispers of wisdom from an old bloke.
Every chapter a rabbit hole dive,
In this fuzzy chaos, we come alive.

Revelations by the Window

Bright sunbeams act like curious spies,
As neighbors argue beneath the skies.
A rubber plant sports a jaunty hat,
While dreams of travel nap on the mat.

The curtains sway to a silent tune,
Eavesdropping on gossip from noon to moon.
Life's truths revealed with each passing car,
In the whirl of the chaos, we're never too far.

Days Spent in Stillness

Time stands still, or so it seems,
In mismatched PJs, we plot our dreams.
The clock ticks loudly, a quirky beat,
As snacks become the day's main treat.

We play board games, but no one wins,
Cheesy jokes hide beneath our grins.
With laughter echoing across the floor,
Stillness dances, and we ask for more.

Transitory Spaces

Socks on the floor, a tumble of fate,
A cat on the couch, debating my state.
Popcorn on the cushions, a movie's lost plot,
Where did it go? Oh wait, I forgot!

The clock ticks away, as we laugh and we snack,
Sticky fingers reach for a late-night attack.
Cushions are mountains, and blankets, a fort,
In this small chaos, we find our report.

Time Stamped in Comforts

The TV hums softly, critiquing my life,
I argue back, with a jest and some strife.
Remote's in the cushions, lost but not missed,
In sitcoms of yore, my worries dismissed.

Chairs with imprints of every remote,
An armrest tribunal for each silly vote.
We plot our shenanigans, laughter ablaze,
Moments enshrined in this quirky haze.

Hugs Wrapped in Fabric

A quilt of odd patterns, stories we weave,
Draped over our shoulders, in warmth we believe.
Mismatched socks lounging, they've lost their way,
Each a lone soldier, who chose to dismay.

The couch, a confessional, spills all our dreams,
Echoing laughter, the ridiculous schemes.
With each sip of tea, we dissolve in delight,
Here in our bubble, the world feels just right.

Half-Empty Mugs of Dreams

Coffee cups scatter like stars in the night,
Each sip a reminder of our playful plight.
Crumbs on the table tell tales of our day,
Map crumbs of laughter, in a colorful way.

A blanket fort towers, declaring its reign,
Guarded by plush toys, the sweetest of pain.
We lose track of time, in this wacky domain,
Where half-empty mugs hold the best kind of gain.

Flickering Hues at Dusk

The cat naps high on the chair,
Dreams of fish in the air.
While the TV blares a tale,
Of a talking bird on a snail.

Lampshades dance, shadows play,
Who knew lamps had such a sway?
A couch may sigh under weight,
Laughing at our junk food fate.

Frame by Frame: Life Within

Photos lined with silly grins,
Captured moments, where to begin?
Each snapshot tells a wild jest,
Like the one with Auntie dressed as a pest.

Snacks spread out, a feast on the floor,
Crumbs tell stories of laughter and more.
In this gallery of our days,
We thrive in quirky, funny ways.

Tales Woven in Cushions

Cushions snug, they hold the tales,
Of spilled drinks and crazy fails.
One's a pirate, one's a king,
In a quest for the ultimate snack thing.

Remote battles, who's in control?
Flipping channels, that's our goal.
With popcorn flying like confetti,
We cheer on our sitcom's petty.

Unraveled Threads of Memory

A quilt of mishaps, stitched with care,
Grandpa lost in his rocking chair.
Grandma's yarn a colorful mess,
Knitting chaos, we all confess.

Beneath the table, a treasure trove,
Of lost socks that no one knows.
Here's to the laughter we find in the day,
In this quirky, funny ballet.

Shadows on the Wall

Shadows dance, as chairs recline,
A cat plots mischief, oh, so divine.
Dust bunnies gather, a fluffy brigade,
While socks go missing in their playful raid.

The lampshade sways in evening's glow,
A dance party starts, with no guests to show.
Remote controls are lost in a race,
While popcorn flies in a buttery chase.

Echoes of Laughter

Jokes are shared with a side of glee,
As Grandma's stories become our spree.
The couch is comfy, a giggle fest,
Where every punchline is truly the best.

Each cushion a fortress, each blanket a shield,
In this kingdom of laughter, our hearts are revealed.
Tickles and chuckles echo off walls,
In this merry room where joy never stalls.

A Corner for Dreams

In the corner, a chair with a flair,
Reading adventures without a care.
Pillow-forts rise like castles of might,
Where imaginations take off and ignite.

The leftover pizza is now gourmet,
While wild tales take us far away.
A treasure chest full of wishes to find,
In this nook where silliness is kind.

The Cozy Confessional

Under a blanket, secrets unfold,
The truth about snacks, just so bold.
Confessions of binge-watching spree,
And who really ate the last cookie, whee!

A laughter-laced moment, a shared delight,
Where spilled drinks are met with pure light.
The walls hold our giggles, our joys, and fears,
In this snug nook, we share our cheers.

The Chronicles of Shared Spaces

In a couch contest, who will win?
The cat's napping in a blanket pin.
Remote wars spark with laughter loud,
While snacks disappear, hidden in a shroud.

Socks reappear in oddest spots,
Under cushions or in flower pots.
A blanket fort built with style and grace,
Turns into a throne, our favorite place.

Dust Motions and Daydreams

Dust bunnies dance like tiny dreams,
Under the coffee table, it seems.
Laughter echoes as we build things,
From cardboard boxes, our kingdom springs.

Daydreaming on a lazy afternoon,
The clock melts slowly, like a tune.
Each sip of tea brings silly thought,
While we plot the schemes we never sought.

Edges of Everyday

In the corners, secrets hide,
A pile of clothes, our scatterbride.
We sip our tea, share silly tales,
Of lost remote controls and ghostly wails.

The dog arranges his favorite spot,
While we argue about the best sitcom plot.
Every bump and laugh marks the time,
Turning life's chaos into a rhyme.

Leaves of Absence

Socks gone rogue, they take their leave,
While the old chair plots how to deceive.
Plants whisper scandals, growing bold,
As the couch reveals secrets untold.

We nestle in dreams that twist and sway,
An afternoon lost in delightful play.
In this hideaway, laughter's the key,
Creating moments, just you and me.

The Symphony of Togetherness

In chaos we gather, a symphony loud,
With snacks on the table and laughter unbowed.
Remote controls fly like a game in the fray,
Who's winning this round? Who's got the say?

Pillow forts rise up, a fortress of dreams,
We're pirates, we're ninjas, or so it seems.
In the corner, the cat plays a starring role,
Catching stray popcorn like it's a goal.

The couch is a ship on an uncharted sea,
Navigated by all, including the bee.
In mismatched pajamas, adventures unfold,
With tales that are silly, and legends retold.

So here's to the antics, the cheers and the jeers,
In a space full of memories, laughter, and cheers.
When friends come together, the magic is clear,
This symphony of chaos, we hold oh so dear.

Crossed Paths and Open Arms

In slippers we shuffle, a dance on the floor,
Trading our stories while we laugh and we snore.
With tea spills and giggles, the night takes a turn,
For wisdom and wit, we have much more to learn.

The dog steals the spotlight, a fur-covered star,
As we pretend we don't see, from close and from far.
Crossed paths through the years, with hugs just the same,
This laughter-filled world, a never-ending game.

The doorbell announces another grand guest,
Who's made a new dish that they claim is the best.
With forks and with spoons, we cheerfully feast,
On flavors that challenge our taste buds' least.

In this crazy haven, we find joy anew,
With crossed paths and open arms to pursue.
So let's raise a glass to these moments we share,
In this comical circus, it's love in the air.

Whispers of Worn Sofas

Cushions sag, a sigh escapes,
Old popcorn stains seem to make,
A throne of crumbs, a royal seat,
Where socks and dreams often meet.

Pet hair whispers in the sun,
A battle lost, a playful run,
Remote control gone on a spree,
It laughs, as do the cats, carefree.

Old magazines stacked high and proud,
Stories spent, yet still too loud,
The clock ticks on, yet we remain,
In our quirky, cozy domain.

Each corner creaks with tales to tell,
Of laughter mingling, quite the swell,
Beneath the lamp, a shadow's play,
In this space where we jest and sway.

Echoes of Absent Laughter

Echoes bounce from wall to wall,
Of jokes retold, a giddy call,
The rug, a witness to the fun,
Where punchlines dance till day is done.

A chair reclines, its back a friend,
It nods along, will never end,
While dust bunnies plot under the light,
With mischief brewing, oh what a sight!

Socks go missing, tales unfold,
In this circus of warmth untold,
We spill our secrets, giggles too,
In each crack and crevice, laughter grew.

The wall clock grins, a timeless jest,
Time's a prankster in its nest,
Yet here we sit, in chuckles bound,
In this space, joy knows no ground.

Shadows in the Corner

Shadows linger in the nooks,
Collectors of our secret looks,
Each chuckle trapped, a fleeting spark,
As tales unfold in laughter's arc.

Underneath a table's maze,
Old toys reminisce their play days,
The lamp flickers, a ghostly grin,
What kind of shenanigans begin?

A blanket fort holds whispers tight,
As socks engage in pillow fights,
While floors bear witness to our schemes,
In friendly rows of silly dreams.

The coffee mug knows all the lore,
With every sip, we crave for more,
In the corners, shadows sway,
With laughter fueling our ballet.

Frayed Edges of Comfort

Frayed edges tell of nights so bright,
When stories soared in giggles light,
A sofa's embrace, plush and wide,
   Holds every secret that we hide.

Mismatched pillows, a quirky sight,
Like friends who always get it right,
Together we plot, we scheme, we dream,
   In laughter's glow, we find our theme.

The coffee maker hums a tune,
While socks unite their grand monsoon,
Crumbs dance upon the wooden floor,
As the clock declares we'll laugh some more.

Each frayed thread clings to a laugh,
The kind that cuts our worries in half,
With every joke, with every cheer,
   In this nest we hold our dear.

A Thousand Stories in Silence

In corners where the dust bunnies play,
Old socks host a dance every Saturday.
The couch whispers tales of the TV wars,
While the cat stares down its invisible foes.

Each cushion a witness to every mishap,
Remote lost in the depths like a treasure map.
Laughter huddles under the coffee table,
Echoes of chaos—the story's fable.

The clock ticks loudly, reminding us when,
Dinner's burnt, but the jokes never end.
We gather round with tales that ignite,
While crumbs gather in the soft evening light.

Cracks in the Paint

Cracks in the paint tell secrets of old,
Of spilled drinks and arguments, heartily bold.
A mustache on the portrait, a work of art,
Reminds us all not to take life to heart.

The coffee stains form constellations now,
As we wonder how socks vanish, yet somehow.
Dust motes swirl like confetti in air,
Celebrating moments that used to ensnare.

A remote confronts a lost battle scene,
Where bickering siblings fought fiercely, unseen.
We laugh at the chaos and the days gone by,
Each crack is a memory, a wink of the eye.

Sipping Joy

Sipping joy from a chipped coffee mug,
Tea leaves swirling like a lovely bug.
Each cup holds stories, some sweet, some wild,
As we raise our glasses like we're all still a child.

The kettle sings songs of warmth and delight,
While the toaster pops up like a morning light.
We toast to the moments that get us through,
Every sip a promise, every laugh brand new.

Chocolates melt like the day's sweet fate,
As we sip on our drinks and procrastinate.
In this room, magic brews in porcelain clay,
With laughter as our guide, we chase blues away.

Hearth Hums and Heartbeats

The hearth hums softly, a warm lullaby,
As we share our dreams before they flutter by.
Heartbeats syncopate to the rhythm of friends,
With each passing moment, the laughter extends.

Footprints of memories scattered on the floor,
Bring back the echoes of laughter and roar.
We cozy up tight with blankets galore,
As the love in this room breaks down every door.

The shadows waltz with whispers of cheer,
In this little abode, we have nothing to fear.
With hearth hums and heartbeats, we weave life's tune,
In this quirky corner, love always blooms.

Echoes of the Unsaid

In corners where laughter hides,
The cat gazes with eyes wide.
Did I say socks should be worn?
Now they're pillows, slightly torn.

A voice calls from the kitchen,
"What's in that dish you're glitchin'?"
A mystery stew, green and swollen,
With flavors that are still unspoken.

Old tales swirl like dust in light,
The couch groans, feeling the bite.
What's that smell? Oh, it's just dissent,
From the broccoli that time forgot, bent.

We laugh at our dining table plight,
Discussing whether fish can sight.
As forks clash and giggles burst,
This room's a circus, for better or worse.

Threads of Connection

A blanket fort, our fortress proud,
With popcorn wars, we laugh out loud.
Who thought pillows could fly so high?
Except for the one that hit my eye.

Remote battles rage with glee,
Choose a show, or war there'll be.
The sofa becomes a ship at sea,
Navigate waves of pure decree.

Each inside joke, a woven thread,
Like tangled yarn, our friendship spread.
We're all part of this silly quilt,
With giggles stitched, our laughter built.

The clock spins as night draws near,
With each strange story, we cheer.
In this cozy space, we unite,
Threads of connection, a joyful sight.

A Canvas of Emotions

Cereal spills artistically bright,
As kids claim breakfast is a fight.
Milk rivers flow on the canvased floor,
While we giggle and reach for more.

Amidst the chaos, crayons collide,
On paper, wild horses reside.
"No, that's a dinosaur in disguise!"
We paint our dreams with bright surprise.

Family debates on color schemes,
Arguments echo, the wildest themes.
Protests arise over purple and green,
An art exhibit like you've never seen.

A masterpiece hangs with pride on display,
Each brush stroke tells us to play.
In this room where chaos swirls,
We create our world, laughter unfurls.

Evening Compositions

As twilight weaves its soft embrace,
We compose symphonies, a silly race.
Who can make the loudest snack crunch?
In this noisy, delightful munch.

Out of tune, the laughter rings,
With each voice, our joy takes wings.
The dog howls to our offbeat song,
As if to join where we belong.

The shadows dance in dimming light,
Compositions of our silly plight.
A missing shoe leads to grand tales,
Connected hearts where laughter prevails.

With every note, our love is clear,
In this room where we hold dear.
We sing our tunes, playful and bright,
Creating memories, our hearts take flight.

A Whirlwind of Memories

Cushions tossed, what a sight,
Remote lost, now we fight.
Laughs echo, game night spree,
Pizza grease on the TV.

Cats parade with fluffy grace,
Whiskers twitch, they own this space.
Soda spills on brand new rug,
Each mishap a warm hug.

Lost the plot, we pause to stare,
Is that a snack, or a lost bear?
Silly stories, stories that shriek,
In our bubble, laughter unique.

Evenings linger, jokes unfold,
In our fortress, we strike gold.
Chasing dreams till morning light,
Memories dance, oh what a night!

Carved in Quietude

Footprints stray on polished wood,
Each corner holds a hidden 'would'.
Sock puppets plot their sweet revenge,
In this place, we all binge.

Tea stains dance on ancient books,
Dust bunnies eye us with their looks.
A chair squeaks, a ghostly sound,
Who knew silence could astound?

Crazy hats line up in rows,
A fashion show, who really knows?
Stories spill from cozy nooks,
Finding joy in quirky hooks.

Nighttime tales spin webs of cheer,
Laughter crackles, all else disappears.
Carved in quiet, our hearts play,
In this haven, we stay and sway.

Harmonies of Home

A blender sings, a kettle hums,
Synchronizing with our fun drums.
Singing socks, a mismatched pair,
Rhythms twirl in the evening air.

Family feuds over board game rules,
Button mashing, oh, such fools!
Last slice of cake, now here's a fight,
Sugar-fueled, we take flight.

Pets perform their breakdance flair,
Chasing tails without a care.
A comedy of errors on display,
Every moment, we laugh away.

Lights dim down, stories unfold,
In the chaos, love we hold.
Harmonies rise, they never tire,
Home is a stage, full of fire!

Flickering Shadows of the Heart

Flickering lights, a candle's glow,
Whispers tell what we all know.
Cartoon voices fill the air,
In this realm, we shed our care.

Slip-n-slides on wooden floors,
Toys explode from hidden drawers.
Silly faces in the frame,
Every shadow knows our name.

Foot races to the fridge we go,
Stale popcorn, how fast it flows!
Jokes and jests, a constant stream,
In our laughter, we find our dream.

Seated snug where warmth resides,
Wrapped in fun, our joy abides.
Flickering moments spark a start,
In this realm, we feel the heart.

Reflections in Each Glance

In the corner sits the cat,
With a look of pure disdain.
Who needs a television?
Her judgment is our gain.

The fridge hums a silly song,
As we gather round to eat.
Forgotten leftovers dance,
Making our meal complete.

A cushion battle starts to brew,
With laughter as our guide.
We throw them like we're pros,
With giggles we can't hide.

Each glance tells a story long,
Of mishaps and of grace.
In this room, our tales run wild,
With smiles upon each face.

Sweaters and Secrets

A raccoon on the TV screen,
Stealing all our snacks.
While Grandma knits a sweater,
That's eight sizes too lax.

Whispers float with spicy tea,
About uncles' dubious hair.
As we try to keep a straight face,
And pretend we do not care.

The dog thinks it's all a game,
With a sock stuck on his head.
He prances like a king,
In his royal, tattered thread.

In this chaos, warmth unfolds,
With secrets tucked away.
Sweaters hold our laughter close,
As dusk turns into play.

Sunbeams and Shadow Play

A sunbeam dances on the wall,
Creating shadows bright.
We mimic them with silly poses,
Our laughter takes flight.

The clock ticks time away from us,
As we lounge with snacks galore.
Who needs to go on grand adventures,
When the couch is our floor?

A pillow fort stands proud and tall,
Against monsters of the day.
We giggle as we guard our keep,
In our own hideaway.

With stories sung in shadow light,
And sunbeams warm and free,
We treasure every silly gleam,
In sweet camaraderie.

The Melodies of Comfort

The kettle whistles a jazzy tune,
As tea swirls in our cups.
We tap our feet to its rhythm,
With pastry crumbs and pups.

A sock puppet joins the jam,
As we laugh 'til we cry.
Impromptu shows unfold,
As we let our spirits fly.

Grandma's stories are our songs,
Of mischief and delight.
Her words a melody so warm,
That lingers through the night.

In this lively concert hall,
We sit and hum along.
With each note wrapped in comfort,
We weave our own sweet song.

Echoes of Everyday Moments

In a corner, the cat sprawls wide,
While the sock monster takes a ride.
Pringles stacked in a teetering tower,
Who knew this could be our finest hour?

TV blares, the kids are loud,
Dad's lost remote becomes a shroud.
Popcorn battles between the clans,
Guess who wins? The dog, of course, his plans!

A plant we named Fred drinks too much,
Leaves dropping, it's losing its touch.
"Just water it!" Mom shouts with glee,
Yet it drinks like it's got a degree!

A couch that swallows all who sit,
"Let's play a game!"—oh, not that bit.
We'll laugh till we can't stand up tall,
In this rumpled chaos, we have it all.

Fragments of Family

Grandma's chair with fabric old,
Holds stories that were once bold.
Kids make forts, and Dad ensures,
That he fits in with all the spurs.

Siblings throw pillows with delight,
Mom yells, "Don't break anything, all right?"
Cousin's laughing, slips and slides,
While the vacuum's stuck where it hides.

Coffee stains on the table's fate,
When 'adulting' is just too late.
Dishes pile; the cats just stare,
In chaos, we find treasures rare.

Every laugh a little fight,
Living here feels just so right.
Though our stories often drift,
These moments are our greatest gift.

A Chair for Every Heart

In our haven, a chair for all,
Big and small, we hear the call.
When the dog jumps, it's quite the sight,
Turns our cozy to a delight.

Mom's on the recliner, painted dreams,
With her book and her chocolate schemes.
Dad's throne is lost in snacks and crumbs,
His favorite seat has seen many runs.

The kids pile in, pushing boundaries,
Creating comfort amidst calamities.
No chair untouched, the pillows fly,
As laughter echoes, spirits fly high.

Every heartbeat fills these chairs,
Frayed edges hold both love and cares.
Amongst the cushions, life's art plays,
In this funny dance, our hearts will stay.

Stains of Time and Tea

A teacup cracked, but none to fret,
Each stain tells a tale we won't forget.
Grandpa's stories steeped in tea,
Laughter bubbles—well, mostly glee!

Fleeting moments, spilled on the floor,
Who knew tea could open such doors?
A scone battle, crumbs in the air,
All while the dog pretends to care.

Old magazines act as time's glue,
Words mingling like tea brews anew.
Every leaf tells who we are,
In gigs and giggles, you're a star!

This den of chaos, cozy and bright,
Holds secrets spun through day and night.
Stains on the table and spills like rain,
In each drop, love and laughter remain.

Dusty Novels and Open Hearts

On the shelf, a book waits, ruffled,
Pages turned, stories all shuffled.
Laughter spills from corners dim,
Plot twists and jokes on a whim.

Old chairs creak with tales unsaid,
A game of charades, a cat leaps ahead.
Distant echoes of laughter rise,
As wisdom fades and humor flies.

Dust motes dance in the soft light,
We share our jokes and hold them tight.
Every spine cracked, every heart free,
Meanwhile, the dog snores in harmony.

Memories, like pages, unfold,
With every laugh, new stories retold.
In this space where we all belong,
Life is a joke, and we sing along.

A Tapestry of Togetherness

Threads of stories weave through air,
Knots of laughter, family care.
Socks mismatched, and tales a-flap,
Games of bingo and a quick nap.

The couch becomes our royal throne,
Where all our quirks can freely be shown.
A mug in hand, and snacks galore,
Who knew our hearts could ask for more?

When dilemmas arise, we just grin,
Solutions found in the chaos within.
With popcorn fights and blanket forts,
We craft a world of joyful sorts.

Every chuckle, a stitch in time,
Woven together, in rhythm and rhyme.
A tapestry rich with colors bright,
In our snuggly space, we find the light.

Shrugging Off the Day

Come dripping in from the world's grey,
We shake off woes, come what may.
In comfy seams and slippers worn,
With silly hats and cushions torn.

The clock strikes six, and laughter swells,
As tales emerge with quirky spells.
Dinner's burnt, but who even cares?
We laugh so hard it's lost in airs.

A book lies open, we're lost in thought,
As droll imagery can't be bought.
Outlandish dreams take flight like birds,
In our realm, no need for words.

With bedtime near, we start to doze,
Drenched in joy, with laughter flows.
In this space, we shake off fraught,
Life's silly dance, now simply wrought.

Patterns of Serenity

In a room where quiet sneaks,
We stumble on as laughter peaks.
With mismatched socks and half-spilled tea,
Serenity flows in our revelry.

Patterns linger on the wall,
Stories whispered, soft and small.
A puzzle piece, lost on the floor,
Where we gather, who needs more?

Cushions piled, a fortress high,
Amid the chaos, a happy sigh.
We share our dreams, both wild and bright,
Finding joy in the softest light.

In each flopped joke and silly tease,
We embrace the lightness, hearts at ease.
Forever stitched in comfort's embrace,
In our cherished nook, we find our place.

Soft Light and Silent Wishes

In the corner sits a cat, so sly,
With dreams of chasing butterflies up high.
The couch is soft, the snacks abound,
Yet none are safe, not even the hound.

The TV hums a long-lost tune,
While chairs creak softly, making room.
We sip our tea and spill some cheer,
The ghost of last week's pizza still near.

A blanket fort made from every sheet,
Our fortress held together by old, cold feet.
We laugh till we snort, it's a glorious sight,
In this cozy chaos, wrong feels right.

Soft light streams, oh what a tease,
As we dodge the crumbs with graceful ease.
Together we plot our snazzy escape,
From the grip of chores, our great escape.

The Art of Stillness

Sitting still, but the clock's in a race,
As squirrels outside put on a chase.
A cup of coffee cooling quite fast,
While my thoughts wander, a wild cast.

What's that smell? Oh no, burnt toast!
It's the breakfast that's turned into a ghost.
With laughter echoing through the air,
We ponder if we should venture to dare.

The dog snorts up, half asleep,
Dreaming of treats and secrets to keep.
Our plans to clean, a fleeting art,
As snacks overwhelm and laughter starts.

In this stillness, chaos brews bright,
An ode to laziness, pure delight.
Each moment's gone before we can blink,
Who knew stillness could lead to mischief and drink?

Remnants of Afternoon Tea

The table's dressed with crumbs and grace,
A treasure map of a sweet embrace.
An empty jar where jam once lay,
Now holds whispers of the day.

Someone's chin rests on a shoe,
Dreaming of snacks like it's a zoo.
Cookies are gone, and so is the silk,
With whispers of laughter as smooth as milk.

A teapot giggles as it holds its brew,
Too weak for the elder but perfect for two.
Honey drips like it knows the secrets,
Found in the laughter and light-hearted regrets.

We sip and sigh, as the sun starts to lean,
While shadows dance in a sweet routine.
Afternoon's glow fades to a gleam,
Leaving behind just a whimsical dream.

Twilight and Togetherness

As twilight blushes, the world feels new,
The lamp flickers, giving a quiet view.
Cozy whispers weave through the air,
While the dog sprawls, too tired to care.

Let's rediscover our lost little games,
Like 'who can sit still'—we're all to blame.
Chasing shadows that refuse to hide,
While the moon chuckles, our silly guide.

Chips on the table act like sentries,
Guarding our giggles, a few secrets, and entries.
With the jar of laughter sitting quite close,
Each joke feels warmer, a delightful dose.

As the world sleeps, we sit side by side,
Finding joy in the mundane, our hearts open wide.
In this twilight moment, we softly agree,
That friendship's the spice in this life's comedy.

The Afternoon Light

Sunbeams dance on dusty floors,
Chasing shadows, opening doors.
Cats flip-flop in the sunny glow,
Dreaming dreams we'll never know.

Cushions stacked in a tall, proud heap,
Unstable towers where children creep.
Giggles burst like bubbles in the air,
Mom's chase for snacks becomes a dare.

Television blares its silly tune,
As socks escape without a rune.
The clock sighs, losing track of time,
While snacks have turned into a crime.

Laughter echoes off the walls,
As popcorn bounces, then it falls.
In this space where joy's unplanned,
The afternoon slips through our hands.

Chronicles of Forgotten Slippers

Two mismatched slippers by the door,
One's a warrior, the other a bore.
They plot and scheme while no one sees,
A grand escape, a soft-breeze tease.

Under the couch, there's a tale to tell,
Of crumbs and dust and a lost key bell.
Adventures in the dark, where they roam,
Will anyone find their way back home?

A dance with the vacuum, slight and quick,
One dodges left, and one plays slick.
Oh, the laughter when they collide,
A fabric feud that won't subside.

In the chaos of everyday life,
They plot their mischief, causing strife.
But when the night calls this wild escapade,
They settle down, and friendships are made.

Conversations in Silence

Staring at walls, with thoughts galore,
What's hidden behind that cupboard door?
Each glance a question, no words to share,
In this quiet dance, there's potential in the air.

The plants eavesdrop on our lost chats,
While dust bunnies settle, entertaining their spats.
Windows watch our lives unfold,
As our secrets intermingle and are retold.

A wink is worth a thousand cries,
As our laughter fills the space, it flies.
Silence breaks, and confusion grows,
Who knew stillness could be so close?

Yet vibrant memories emerge like blooms,
In this room that holds our weary looms.
With every hiccup in this calm stream,
We craft our stories, punctured by dream.

Breathing in the Quiet

In the stillness, a dust motes waltz,
Whispering secrets, like gentle faults.
Coffee brews in a quiet hum,
While behind us, the world's become numb.

A sleepy cat sprawls over the chair,
Dreaming of mice that lead to nowhere.
The clock ticks softly, a rhythmic tune,
As we plan our next wild afternoon.

Books piled high, a leaning tower,
Each spine a promise, each page a power.
Here we linger, lost in the haze,
As minutes drip through a sunlit maze.

This cozy corner, a quiet retreat,
Breathe in the silence; it's life's little treat.
Laughing at nothing, we aim for the sky,
In this cozy bubble, time has no tie.

A Tapestry of Memory

In the corner, a chair squeaks,
As Uncle Bob tells his jokes.
Laughter spills like spilled drinks,
While the dog makes playful pokes.

Grandma's quilt, a patchwork tale,
Of all the family's oddest quirks.
Cousins argue who's more frail,
Over who did the best works.

A cat leaps onto the snack tray,
Claiming the chips as her throne.
Everyone pauses to say,
"Did anyone hear a groan?"

With each sip of tea we share,
Memories twist like pretzel bends.
In this space, free of despair,
Our laughter is how the time bends.

Candles Flicker

Candles flicker, shadows play,
As stories weave in hushed tones.
A sock puppet steals the day,
With antics that reign like drones.

A game of charades unfolds,
With gestures that make no sense.
Someone yells, "I'm pure gold!"
While others just laugh and commence.

The couch hides crumbs, quite the hauler,
A whisper of secrets concealed.
Dad trips over in a brawler,
"To the vet!" is all that he squealed.

Through giggles, we find our way,
In this cocoon of heart and cheer.
As wax drips, and night turns day,
Each memory holds us near.

Stories Unfold

In the fabric of the night,
Stories unfold, one by one.
Grandpa's tales, a true delight,
All end with laughter, not done.

The clock ticks in mellow sync,
While Aunt Sue spills milk with flair.
"Not a drop!," we all distinctly think,
As she wipes it off her hair.

Nostalgia dances like a breeze,
Through the family quilt we weave.
From funny mishaps to shared tease,
In these moments, we believe.

With each chuckle, we get bolder,
As secrets simmer and stew.
In this room, warmth's a holder,
Each story is a bond known true.

Portraits of Togetherness

In the frames, our faces grin,
Like goofy statues set in time.
With mischief, we start to spin,
Every moment, we dare to climb.

Sister steals the last donut,
While we plot her sweet revenge.
Coffee brews, but looks are shut,
Laughter bends around the edge.

The TV's on, and nobody sees,
The plot twist defended with glee.
While dogs play rough with such ease,
Forming their own comedy spree.

Together, we rewrite each scene,
Of life's absurd and joyful tales.
In our hearts, a space for the keen,
These portraits, love never fails.

The Dusty Coffee Table Tales

On the coffee table, dust resides,
Among the things we hold so dear.
Every trinket, a secret hides,
Echoes of laughter we hear.

A remote, three years overdue,
From the last great movie night.
A snack bowl, with popcorn stew,
Reminds us, it was quite a sight.

Magazines piled, old and frayed,
With tales of fashion far from now.
"Who wore it best?" a joke well-played,
As everyone stumbles to wow.

With drinks raised high amidst the mess,
Each sip unlocks a new cheer.
In our huddle, we feel the bless,
Collecting moments we hold dear.

The Mirror's Reflection

In the mirror, I see my hair,
A wild creature, beyond compare.
It laughs at me, with all its might,
As I attempt to tame it right.

The toothpaste fights a daily war,
It splatters smiles from the bathroom floor.
My socks have vanished, it's a crime,
It's like they went for a fun time.

I dance like no one's here to see,
But the cat just watches, judging me.
He pretends to be unimpressed,
While I strut my stuff, feeling blessed.

Each moment spent, a funny tale,
In this mirror, I'll never fail.
With every glance, I'm met with glee,
A vibrant life, just me and me.

Solace Found Between Pillows

Lost in a sea of fluffy dreams,
Between the pillows, laughter beams.
The dog thinks he's the king tonight,
As I wrestle for a spot, what a sight!

The popcorn bowl's now a treasure,
Dispersed in chaos, purest pleasure.
We giggle at our nightly feast,
As crumbs draw in a furry beast.

Remote control, that slippery friend,
It's hiding again, just won't blend.
We search beneath the cushions wide,
There's a stale chip, we both decide.

With every toss, we find delight,
As shadows dance in soft moonlight.
Pillow fights, our evening thrill,
Moments of joy that time will fill.

Gathering of Moments

Every Sunday, chaos reigns,
The kids run wild, ignoring chains.
Grandma laughs, her cookies fly,
While Uncle Joe attempts to pry.

There's a game of cards, oh so fierce,
With rivalries that none can pierce.
The dog steals snacks when we're not near,
We're left to chase him without fear.

The stories told, some tall, some not,
Of how last year, we caught a slot.
The fish that got away, it grew,
Now it's a whale, did you hear too?

Goodbye to silence, welcome cheer,
In moments shared, we hold so dear.
As laughter echoes, time stands still,
These gatherings, they always thrill.

Serenade of the Surroundings

In the corner, a plant sings low,
Its leaves rustle, just to show.
With sunlight dancing on each frond,
It keeps secrets, of a world beyond.

The clock ticks loud, a metronome,
Each 'tick' says, 'You're close to home.'
While dust bunnies waltz around,
In our hearts, joy knows no bound.

The couch reclines, a throne of rest,
Where every nap feels like the best.
A blanket fort rises in retreat,
Our laughter fills this cozy seat.

So here we sit, in warmth and cheer,
The serenade of life is clear.
In every corner, tales we weave,
In our happy nook, we truly believe.

Seasons of Comfort

The couch is a throne, but where's my snack?
My dog steals the blanket, it's quite the hack.
Remote's gone rogue, hidden deep in the seams,
Across the room, I plot my snack heist dreams.

Winter brings blankets, we pile on the heat,
Summer's fierce sun makes us shuffle our feet.
Spring's sneaky pollen gives me a sneeze scare,
Fall's pumpkin spice lattes, oh the love we share!

Guests come and go, it's a merry parade,
Tripping on shoes that a guest might have laid.
Board games erupt into battles of pride,
Who knew that old Monopoly could incite wide-eyed?

The stories we spin, like a yarn in the air,
The laughter erupts, it's a comic affair.
This room holds the chaos, the joy, and the mess,
Here's to our sanctuary, we couldn't care less!

Fragmented Myths

In a corner, a cat, with a regal pose,
Watching me closely as my snack stash flows.
A tale of a hero who lost at charades,
While villains just laugh at the time that invades.

Socks on the floor, who knew it could be,
The start of a saga, an epic decree?
A kingdom of crumbs where the kings are the crumbs,
Beware of the couch; it's the land of the plums!

Suddenly, a scare from the vacuum's roar,
The stories they make, oh! They never bore.
Grandpa's wild tales of his youth on a bike,
Lead to my own flips—oh boy, that's quite a hike!

With laughter as fuel and the munchies in tow,
Our myths turn to legends, they heighten the glow.
In every corner lies a quest to unwrap,
Funny times linger like a cozy nap.

A Sanctuary of Stillness

Cushions stacked high, like a fort of delight,
Kids play their games, till we vanish from sight.
Fortifications strong, rules of pillow and bed,
In this tiny kingdom, we make fun instead.

Quiet moments linger, with giggles and sighs,
A pause in the chaos, a sweet bond that ties.
Lunch breaks in stealth as we sneak in a bite,
The stealthiest munchies—oh, what a delight!

TV flickers low, the world's outside whirls,
Here we craft stories, adorned with soft pearls.
A slice of calm wrapped in laughter and grace,
This space is our refuge, our sanctuary place.

Even in silence, the love does not end,
With glances exchanged, old wounds we can mend.
In the stillness, joy blooms, and we understand,
This cozy corner is our unspoken land.

Soft Grounded Echoes

Echoes of laughter dance off the walls,
Chasing away shadows, where good humor calls.
A dance in the kitchen with mismatched socks,
Here's where we find all the strange paradox.

Whispers of secrets as we plot our next scheme,
Cookies go missing, but who's to redeem?
Each joke is a brick in this building of glee,
A fortress of happiness, oh, just you and me.

The spilled drink disaster, a laughable plight,
A valiant rescue with towels in sight.
Through antics and tales, what a vibrant spree,
In our little haven, we're wild and carefree.

Silence may dawn, with the night drawing near,
Yet echoes of joy linger, never in fear.
The moments we cherish are woven with thread,
Soft grounded echoes dance on, we're fed.

Beneath the Cozy Blanket

Beneath the blanket, snacks abound,
Crisps and crumbs all over the ground.
As I dig deep, my phone does ping,
It's a meme war—let the laughter ring!

Chasing the cat, she leaps on my head,
In this circus, I'm the jester instead.
With popcorn flying, the only rule,
Is no one leaves till they've lost their cool!

The couch is a ship, sailing the seas,
Gathering stories, like dust on the knees.
Old sitcoms playing, we quote every line,
Laughing so hard, we forget about time!

So here we gather, friends side by side,
Wrapped in laughter, on this cozy ride.
Beneath the blanket, life's a delight,
Turning the mundane into pure laughter's flight!

Mirrors of the Mind

In a world where thoughts roam free,
My brain's a mirror reflecting me.
I asked it kindly, "What's your plan?"
It showed me dancing like a silly man!

Every reflection sparks a giggle,
Like a puppy who loves to wiggle.
Ideas bounce like a trampoline,
Jumping high, it's a comical scene!

When boredom comes to call my name,
I play charades and forget my shame.
Mirrors of laughter, they twist and bend,
A funhouse where the silliness won't end!

So let's embrace this wacky ride,
With a wink and a smirk, we'll take it in stride.
In this mind of mirrors, our joy unconfined,
We find the funny in every kind!

Flickering Flames and Fables

The flames dance lightly, tales in the air,
Of dragons and knights, but we've lost the flair.
I tell a story, and it cracks like a whip,
Yet all my friends roll their eyes and sip.

The marshmallows toast, and so do our dreams,
Each tale getting wilder, or so it seems.
A story of socks that run from the wash,
Together we laugh—oh my, what a nosh!

Fables of giants who can't find their hats,
Or fish that wear bowties, flaunting like chaps.
With every flicker, laughter ignites,
In this cozy corner, our joy takes flight!

So bring on the flames and sprinkle the fun,
Fables unravel till the night is done.
In this glow of stories, we twinkle and flare,
Turning our bumbles into witty fare!

Envelopes of Emotions

Envelopes stacked high with unspoken feels,
Open one up, and let laughter seal.
A letter of joy, a postcard of grins,
The funny side of life is where love begins!

Inside each envelope, secrets abound,
From silly mishaps to joy that astounds.
A note from last Tuesday about spilled ice cream,
We all burst out laughing, it's a shared dream!

The stamps may be quirky, the ink often smudged,
Every page tells a tale, emotions nudged.
From giggles to snorts, we document our days,
In a scrapbook of fun, in silly ways!

So let's cherish these envelopes, one by one,
Filled with the laughter, we've gathered for fun.
In the chaos of life, we hold on tight,
To every silly moment that brings us delight!

Laughter's Lasting Imprint

In the midst of toys and messy chairs,
The laughter echoes, fills the air.
We trip on shoes, a daily scene,
Who knew chaos could feel so serene?

With cookies crumbling on the floor,
We share our secrets, and then some more.
Each spilled drink tells a tale,
Of wild antics that never fail.

The dog thinks he's part of the crew,
Soaking up giggles, a comedy too.
Pillow fort castles, our laughter rings,
In this strange realm, we're all kings.

Memories stuck like gum on a shoe,
Each chuckle leaves an imprint anew.
With every blunder and silly spill,
We find the joy, and that's the thrill.

A Corner for Every Dream

In the corner sits the old guitar,
Dusty dreams beneath a shooting star.
We strum out notes that make us grin,
As the cat yawns wide, joining the din.

A stack of pillows, oh what a sight,
Where superheroes take flight each night.
Imagination soars, the world is vast,
In this cozy nook, time cannot pass.

Remote controls become magic wands,
As we fight dragons, create our bonds.
Popcorn spills fly like confetti rain,
Laughter bundled in every refrain.

A forgotten sock? It's a treasure chest,
Unveiling giggles that never rest.
In this corner where dreams collide,
We dive deep into joy, with hearts open wide.

Whispers of the Sofa

The sofa creaks, a gentle sigh,
Sharing tales while we giggle and try.
Remote battles turn into great wars,
Cuddling tight while dodging popcorn showers.

With every cushion, a story unfolds,
Of laughable mishaps and secrets untold.
The dog snores deep, dreaming absurd,
While we plot our next ridiculous word.

Invisible monsters under the seat,
We laugh out loud, can't stay in our seats.
Sipping fizzy drinks, we raise a toast,
To the sofa that's loved the very most.

In whispers and chuckles, we find our tune,
Beneath the glow of the lazy afternoon.
With every giggle and every shout,
In this space of joy, we never doubt.

Coffee Stains and Conversations

The table's marked with coffee rings,
Tales of mishaps and silly flings.
Laughter bubbles up with every sip,
Staining the day with a joyful trip.

Our mugs are full, spilling over joy,
As we joke about childhood, oh what ploys!
With each little spill, a story brews,
Crafted in giggles and friendly views.

Spoons stirring mischief in our cups,
While we labor to escape hiccup-ups.
In a sea of laughter, we drift and flow,
Warmed by the chaos of the love we know.

The coffee cools, but the smiles won't fade,
In our circle of comfort, the best memories made.
Through sips and spills, we connect and share,
With coffee stains marking the love in the air.

Midnight Musings

In the still of night, a snack I crave,
Chocolate chips and crumbs, my midnight wave.
The fridge hums soft, a comforting tune,
As I dance with snacks under the quiet moon.

My couch, a throne, with cushions so grand,
Remote in hand, I am king of this land.
But oh, what is that? A stray sock has flown,
My kingdom's at risk, my comfort overthrown.

Pillow fights break out, it's me versus sleep,
In this epic battle, I make a mighty leap.
The cat looks on, judging every move,
While the endless reruns invite me to snooze.

But laughter erupts as I trip on a shoe,
The midnight snack dreams start to bid adieu.
With crumbs on my shirt and a smile on my face,
I settle back down in this cozy space.

The Diary of a Dust Bunny

In the corner lies a fluff ball of dust,
With tales of crumbs and soda pop rust.
I whisper my secrets to the feline brigade,
As we plot to invade the night's masquerade.

"Remember the pizza from '93?" I sigh,
"A slice that rolled under, oh my, oh my!"
The laughter rings out, we reignite the past,
As the vacuum cleaner looms, our fun won't last.

We dance through the shadows, bold and carefree,
Chasing old spiders, oh what glee!
A pillow fort fortress can't keep us contained,
In this tumultuous world, we're proudly unchained.

But then the lights flicker, a challenge draws near,
The dreaded machine, it's time to disappear.
We scatter like whispered secrets in the night,
'Til the next great adventure brings us back to the light.

Remnants of Rainy Days

Outside the window, the raindrops tap,
Inside, I'm wrapped in a soft, cozy nap.
A mug of hot chocolate, marshmallows afloat,
My world's an adventure, just like a boat.

Should I build a fortress, all pillows and sheets?
Or maybe a maze of colorful treats?
The cat takes a leap, as if on a quest,
While I ponder which idea is simply the best.

The thunder rolls in, a booming applause,
Each rumble so loud, I giggle because
It sounds like the ceiling is starting to dance,
As I throw caution to winds in a wild trance.

After hours of fun, as the storm starts to fade,
I gather the remnants, my snug fort displayed.
With laughter and cocoa, a place to behold,
The rainy day magic, forever retold.

Playlists and Pillow Forts

With a playlist blasting, my dance moves arise,
In my fortress of pillows, I'm queen of the skies.
Each beat, a reminder that life's just a game,
As I spin like a whirlwind, losing all shame.

The cat joins the party, chasing my feet,
Dancing from sunshine to shadows in heat.
Music blares loud, we shake and we sway,
In our little universe, we'll play all day.

The snacks are aplenty, from popcorn to chips,
I shudder to think how it's gone to my hips!
But laughter erupts with each tune that we sing,
With joy in our hearts, we embrace everything.

So here's to the moments, both silly and bright,
In pillow fort kingdoms, we dance through the night.
With playlists and giggles, our spirits run free,
In this cheerful realm, it's just my cat and me.

Moments in the Margins

In the nook where dust bunnies dance,
A couch cushions giggle, catch a chance.
Socks are tangled, lost in the fray,
The dog stares, plotting his play.

Chips crunch loudly, a daring crunch,
As laughter floats in a chipmunk bunch.
Remote wars break out, who will win?
With a flick of the wrist, let the games begin.

Wine glasses chatter, spill their tales,
Of epic fails and bodacious gales.
The cat thrones high, surveying the mess,
In this crowded kingdom, we are all blessed.

Here in this space, chaos reigns true,
A blend of mayhem, laughter, and brew.
Memories forged in comfy embrace,
In margins of life, we find our place.

Murmurs from the Corners

Whispers drift from the patchy rug,
A secret revealed: an old, cozy mug.
The clock ticks loudly, judging our time,
As we share giggles, sips, and some rime.

The curtains quiver like shy little mice,
As tales of the day unravel our spice.
Pillow forts stand like mighty old ships,
While popcorn pops with excited little skips.

Games of charades spark comedic flair,
Funny faces met with a laugh to share.
The plants all nod, they're part of the throng,
In this corner world, we all belong.

From shadows they chant, good vibes galore,
In whispered tones, they plead for more.
As laughter crescendos, mirth flies high,
In this room of secrets, we never say goodbye.

Just Beyond the Threshold

Step inside where tall tales rise,
With mismatched chairs and quirky highs.
The welcome mat smiles, a well-worn friend,
In this joyous realm, fun finds no end.

A blanket fortress, a beacon of mirth,
Where gaming glory defines our worth.
Lost in a comic, we giggle and squeal,
Every page turn, a delightful reveal.

Potato chips crumbs on the soft, warm seat,
As our laughter dances to a buttery beat.
Bubble tea swirls as secrets unfold,
With sips of joy, we're all stories told.

Through the door, sunlight spills with grace,
Illuminating this happy place.
In corners and cracks, fun's all around,
In this feast of laughter, forever we're bound.

Signs of Togetherness

A pile of laundry, a game with a name,
Who'll find the socks? It's all just the same.
Jokes fly like confetti, float through the air,
In this messy kingdom, we giggle and share.

The cat's perched aloof while napkins take flight,
Saucers and spoons join in the delight.
TV shows blare, but we talk through the din,
In a jumble of joy, we cherish our win.

Remote control battles, who switched the channel?
Stirring the pot, like a comedian's panel.
Caught in the moment, we clink and we cheer,
In this bountiful space, love's loud and clear.

Amid chaos and chuckles, warmth we find,
In the heart of the mess, our lives intertwine.
Tales told with laughter, a riotous mix,
In these signs of togetherness, we thrive in the fix.

Yarn of the Present

In a corner, socks unite,
Missing partners, what a sight!
Cats eyeing yarn with pure delight,
While I ponder my laundry plight.

Chairs that squeak and creak like ghosts,
Friends arrive to share our hosts.
With snacks and laughter, we can boast,
Tales as tall as buttered toast.

Forgotten remotes, lost in the fray,
Under cushions, they choose to stay.
I swear they plot to make me pay,
In this circus of a perfect day.

Light bulbs flicker in a dance,
While kids search for that last toy chance.
Every story, a wild romance,
In this room, we all prance!

Tides of Time

Coffee cups stacked high like towers,
Time slips by in fleeting hours.
Socks disappear under chairs' powers,
In this funny world, laughter showers.

When the news is on, who's really sane?
We cheer the villains, relish pain.
Remote in hand, it's all a game,
With every twist, we scream their name.

Board games sprawled like battle fields,
With missing pieces, yet hope yields.
A house of fun that never shields,
From all the laughter life wields.

As day turns night, the tales arise,
We share old jokes, tend to reprise.
In this room, under all these skies,
We're tangled in our sweet goodbyes.

Illumination of Imaginations

Bright colors splash on every wall,
A canvas of chaos, we embrace it all.
Echoes of laughter rise and fall,
In this quirky space, we hear the call.

Pillows like clouds, we sink into dreams,
Reality bends, or so it seems.
With wild ideas, we break the seams,
In this room, igniting beams.

Pets plotting mischief, oh what a sight!
Chasing shadows in soft twilight.
Each corner hides a little fright,
Yet our giggles soar, oh what a flight!

We gather 'round, enacting plays,
With silly voices, we spend our days.
In our imagination's haze,
Every moment is a bright bouquet.

Fleeting Messages

Post-it notes on the fridge so bright,
Remind me to call, to cook, to write.
Yet somehow, they get lost from sight,
In this whirlwind of joy and slight.

The cookies vanish before they cool,
Kids giggle in the backyard pool.
Every mishap feels like a rule,
In this living room, we're all a fool.

Voices echo from room to room,
With tales of mystery, laughter, and gloom.
Each "You won't believe!" ignites the bloom,
In this chaos, we find our loom.

As twilight drapes its soft embrace,
We swap stories, no time to waste.
In this haven, love finds its place,
A patchwork of memories we trace.

Reflections on the Wall

A mirror holds my silly face,
While the cat makes her regal space.
I pose in outfits that don't quite match,
Laughing till I'm ready to hatch.

My hat collection, somewhat grand,
Sits haphazardly, unplanned.
Guest after guest, they try each one,
Funniest moments—oh, what a run!

Painted landscapes, I take no blame,
With colors bright, it's all a game.
They smile down, with eyes so wide,
At all my quirks, I take in pride.

The wall clocks tick, but I've lost track,
Of how many times I've spilled my snack.
Laughter echoes, the kind so sweet,
In this space where joy and humor greet.

Where Hopes Gathered

My couch is a throne, or so I claim,
With snacks and shows, oh what a fame!
Days drift by, I'm stuck in the fluff,
Dreams float by, but never enough.

A coffee table stacked high with mess,
Hopes spilled out, I must confess.
Each cup tells a tale, each lid a lie,
As popcorn fights to soar and fly.

Friends poke fun at my favorite chair,
"Is it a time machine?" they joke and stare.
Each crease holds memories and sighs,
With laughter ringing, like joyful cries.

In this nook where wishes blend,
Life rolls on, around the bend.
Here's to hope and giggles galore,
In every moment, who could ask for more?

Secrets Beneath the Cushions

Beneath the cushions, treasures hide,
Lost TV remotes and crumbs supplied.
I reach in deep, what will I find?
A half-eaten cookie? Who's so unkind?

Deep in the sofa, echoes my laugh,
Funny notes from my past, what a gaffe!
Friend's doodles and secrets abound,
In this plush world where humor's found.

Every bounce springs new delight,
With stories shared that fly like kite.
The couch has seen every tear and cheer,
So we keep it warm, year after year.

As I dig deeper for just one coin,
I find hilarious things I disjoin.
Well, here's a sock! A mystery so grand,
This space is a carnival, oh how it's planned!

Faded Patterns and Bright Dreams

The rug is frayed, a silly mess,
Yet colorful stains hold laughs, no less.
Dancing patterns made by feet,
Tell stories of joy, bittersweet.

Faded floral becomes my stage,
As I twirl and prance, setting my age.
With every step, the fibers sigh,
"More whirling giggles," I can't deny.

The coffee stains, oh, here they flow,
Like a treasure map of my ebb and glow.
Every spill a comedy routine,
In this space, I reign supreme.

Bright dreams flicker, like TV lights,
Chasing giggles through cozy nights.
In faded corners, life's hues blend,
Creating a tale that will never end.

www.ingramcontent.com/pod-product-compliance
Lightning Source LLC
Chambersburg PA
CBHW070305120526
44590CB00017B/2565